A JOURNEY TO THE BOTTOM OF THE SEA

DOWN
DOWN
DOWN

HATCHET FISH

VIPERFISH

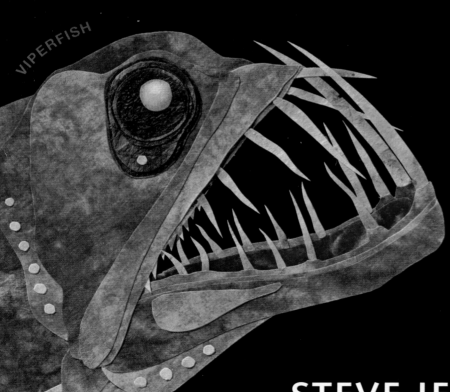

STEVE JENKINS

HOUGHTON MIFFLIN HARCOURT
BOSTON   NEW YORK

For my mother —S.J.

www.hmhco.com

The text of this book is set in Helvetica Neue.
The illustrations are cut-and-torn-paper collage.

The Library of Congress has cataloged the hardcover edition as follows:
Jenkins, Steve, 1952–
Down, down, down: a journey to the bottom of the sea/by Steve Jenkins.
p. cm.
1. Marine animals—Juvenile literature. 2. Deep-sea animals—Juvenile literature. I. Title.
QL122.2.J46 2009
591.799—dc22
2008036082

ISBN: 978-0-618-96636-3 hardcover
ISBN: 978-0-544-70951-5 paperback

Manufactured in China
SCP 13 12 11 10 9 8

4500818833

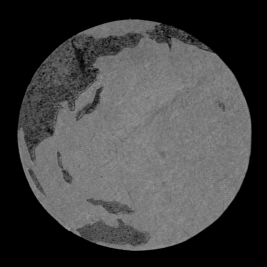

Viewed from space, the earth looks like a watery blue ball. Oceans cover more than two-thirds of the globe's surface, and well over half the planet lies beneath water more than a mile (1½ kilometers) deep. We have explored only a small fraction of the oceans. In fact, more humans have walked on the moon than have visited the deepest spot in the sea.

In this book, we'll descend from the ocean's surface to the sea floor and travel through one of the most extreme environments on earth. Along the way we'll encounter some unusual creatures. You can find out more about these animals at the back of the book.

Above the Surface

Here, just above the surface of the western Pacific Ocean, the air is warm. Below us gentle swells move across the water. It's calm now, but during a storm powerful winds can churn the surface into mountainous waves. The Pacific Ocean is the largest body of water on the planet, with an area greater than all the earth's dry land combined. At this spot the water is more than 13,000 feet (4,000 meters) deep.

Most life on land is found in a zone only a few hundred feet thick, from the tops of the trees to just beneath the ground. The oceans, on the other hand, average two and a half miles (4 kilometers) in depth. They are home to the vast majority of living things on our planet. The water below us teems with life. Sometimes, without warning, the creatures of this hidden world burst into our own . . .

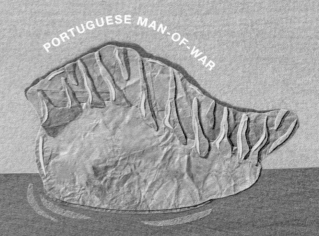

PORTUGUESE MAN-OF-WAR

ALBATROSS

DEEPEST SPOT
IN THE OCEAN

35,838 FEET
(10,923 METERS)

Out of the Water

They may be pursuing prey, escaping danger, or sending a message to others of their kind. Whatever the reason, sea creatures sometimes leap from the water into the air. A huge shark, surging upward to grab its prey, lands with a splash that could empty a swimming pool. A small, sleek squid barely misses us as it shoots by, slipping back into the water with barely a ripple. Other creatures break the surface as well . . .

GREAT WHITE SHARK

FLYING SQUID

SPINNER DOLPHIN

FLYING FISH

MACKEREL

**10 FEET
(3 METERS)
73° F (23° C)**

KRILL

It's a Small World

Near the surface the water is warm and brightly lit by the sun. Light-loving plants, algae, and bacteria — most single-celled and too small to see with the naked eye — are found here in uncountable numbers. Almost all life in the sea depends on these microscopic organisms, which use the sun's energy to help them manufacture their own food. They themselves are food for billions of animals, including shrimplike krill. Krill and other small organisms that drift along with ocean currents are called plankton. Mackerel and other fish gather in enormous schools to feed on plankton.

Big Fish Eat Little Fish

At a depth of just 33 feet (10 meters), the sunlight is already beginning to fade. The pressure is increasing. When we are above the surface, the weight of the air over our heads presses on every part of our bodies. This pressure isn't noticeable unless it changes, as when our ears pop in a fast elevator ride. Water is much heavier than air, and already the pressure has reached two atmospheres — twice what we experience out of the water. We are about as deep as most humans can dive without scuba gear.

Life flourishes here. Large, fast-swimming predators eat smaller fish, herding them together into large swirling balls. Seabirds, some capable of diving to depths of 220 feet (67 meters), attack from above. Other animals feed on seaweed or jellyfish.

GREEN SEA TURTLE

MOLA MOLA

Filter Feeders

Not all large fish are fast-swimming hunters. Both the whale shark, the world's largest fish, and the gigantic manta ray feed directly on plankton. They strain tiny plants and animals from the water passing over their gills. These filter feeders follow swarms of plankton from the surface to depths of several hundred feet. Jellyfish and many other smaller animals are also filter feeders, trapping plankton with sticky tentacles or netlike antennae.

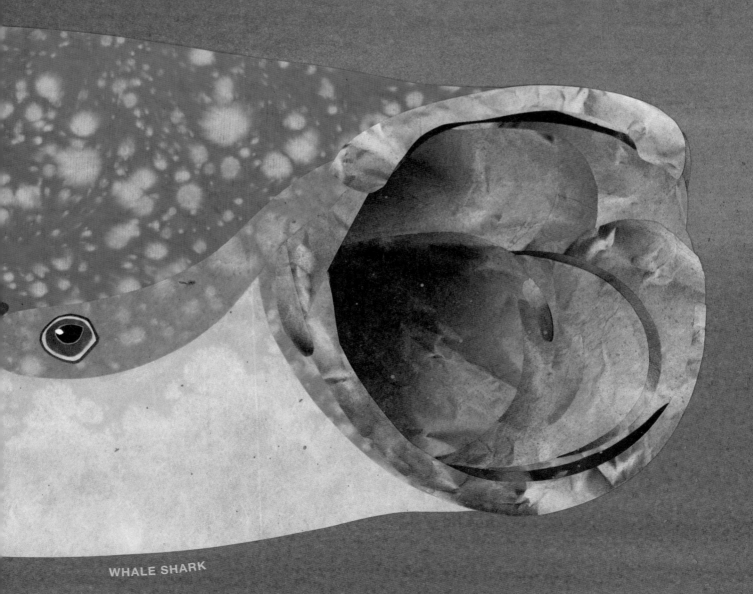

WHALE SHARK

164 FEET
(50 METERS)
72° F (22° C)

MANTA RAY

COMPASS JELLYFISH

Soft Bodies

The light is fading, and the pressure is now ten atmospheres — ten times as great as at the surface. Unlike air, water and other fluids don't compress much, or get smaller, under pressure. The bodies of most ocean animals are filled with fluid, so they don't have a problem with the pressure. Anything containing a hollow, air-filled space, such as a human body or a submarine, risks being crushed as it descends.

Jellyfish are common here. Comb jellies — a family of soft-bodied, transparent animals distantly related to jellyfish — are also plentiful. Jellyfish and comb jellies lack a brain, eyes, and a sense of smell. But they are efficient predators, capturing plankton and small fish with tentacles and sticky bodies. They rise from the depths at night to feed, returning to the safety of deeper water at dawn.

GIRDLE OF VENUS COMB JELLY

Visitors from the Deep

The twilight zone begins about 660 feet (200 meters) below the surface. From here on down, there is not enough light for plants to survive — only animals live below this depth. To us it appears completely dark, but many of the creatures here have eyes that are specially adapted to the faint light. The sunlit waters, with their rich variety of life, are just above us. Animals that are rarely seen at the surface rise from deeper waters to hunt in the twilight zone.

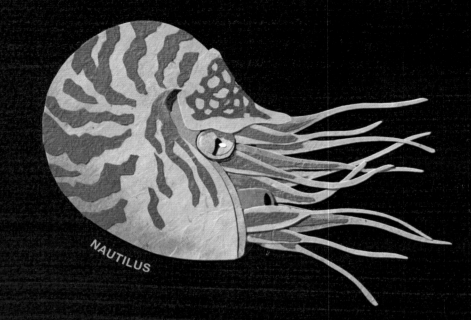

NAUTILUS

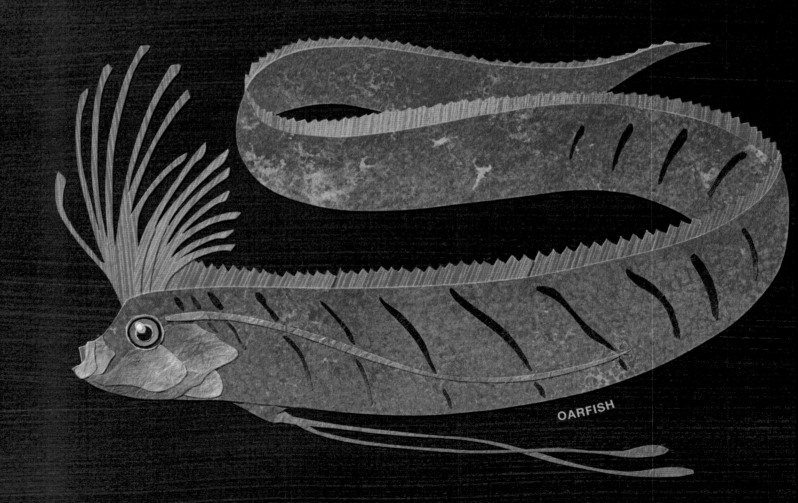

OARFISH

660 FEET
(200 METERS)
68° F (20° C)

GOBLIN SHARK

SNIPE EEL

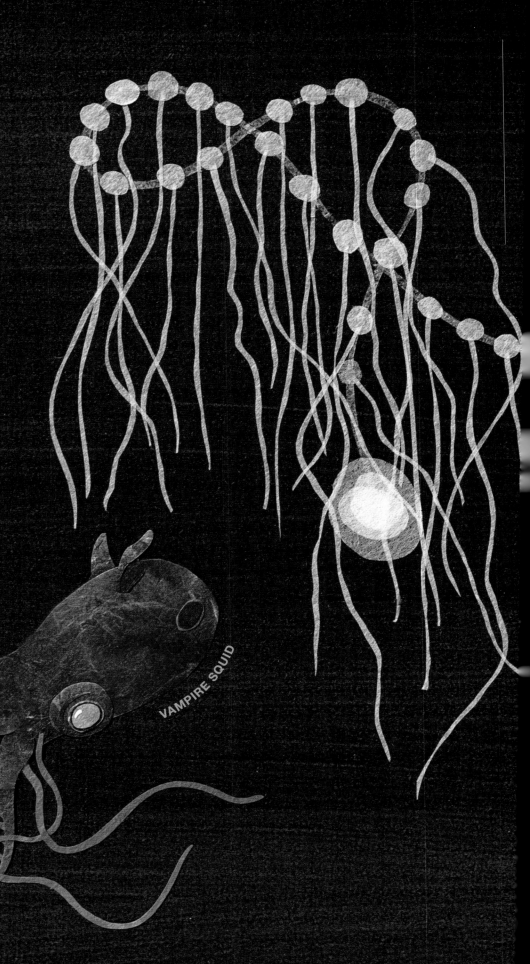

Glowing in the Dark

Nine of every ten animals that live below the sunlit layer of the ocean are bioluminescent (*by-oh-**loo**-muh-**nes**-uhnt*) — they can produce their own light. Animals use bioluminescence to lure prey, confuse or startle attackers, or make themselves difficult to see. Animals also use light to attract a mate or send messages to one another. Because the ocean is so large and so many animals live here, bioluminescence is the most common form of animal communication on earth. Only the slightest glimmer of sunlight reaches this depth, and only animals with extraordinarily sensitive eyes can detect it.

VAMPIRE SQUID

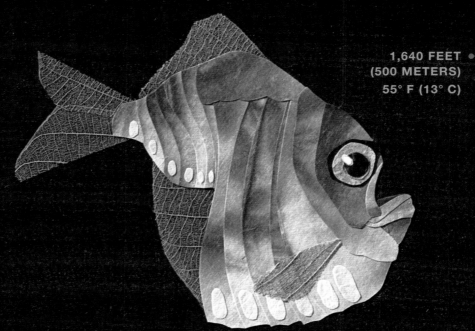

HATCHET FISH

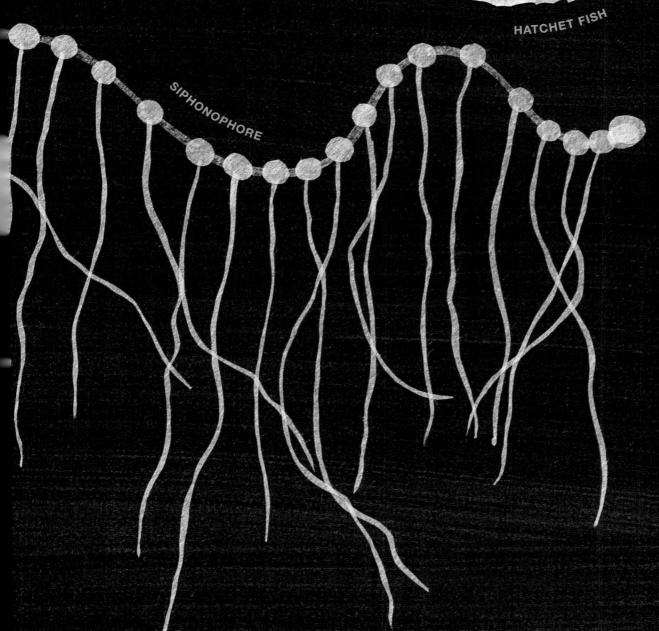

SIPHONOPHORE

1,640 FEET
(500 METERS)
55° F (13° C)

Lights Out

We can see the animals living in these dark waters because we've brought along a light of our own. Without it, we'd see nothing but blackness and the flicker and flash of animal bioluminescence. If we turn off our light, the scene on the previous pages might look something like this . . .

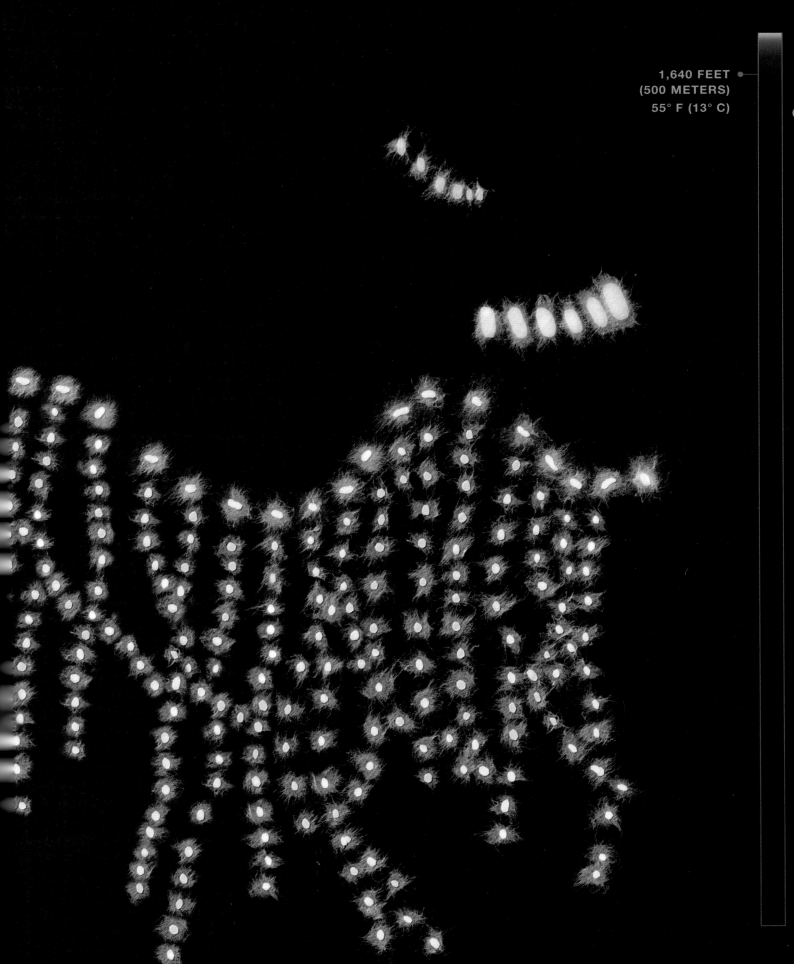

1,640 FEET
(500 METERS)
55° F (13° C)

It's Snowing!

We've reached the dark zone. Not even the faintest sunlight can reach us here. It's getting colder, and the pressure is enormous. Few submarines can dive this deep without being crushed.

All around us a delicate "marine snow" is falling. It's composed of dead plankton, fish scales, animal waste, and bits of larger creatures that have died in the waters above. These particles are the basis of life here. Small animals feed on marine snow and become prey for larger hunters.

PELICAN EEL

PRAM BUG

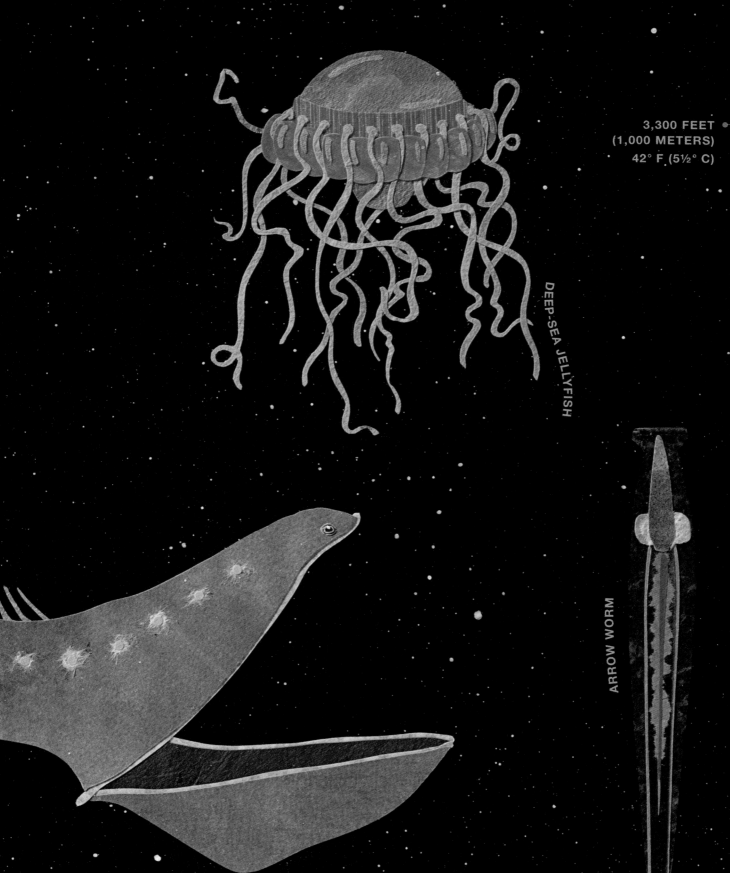

3,300 FEET
(1,000 METERS)
42° F (5½° C)

DEEP-SEA JELLYFISH

ARROW WORM

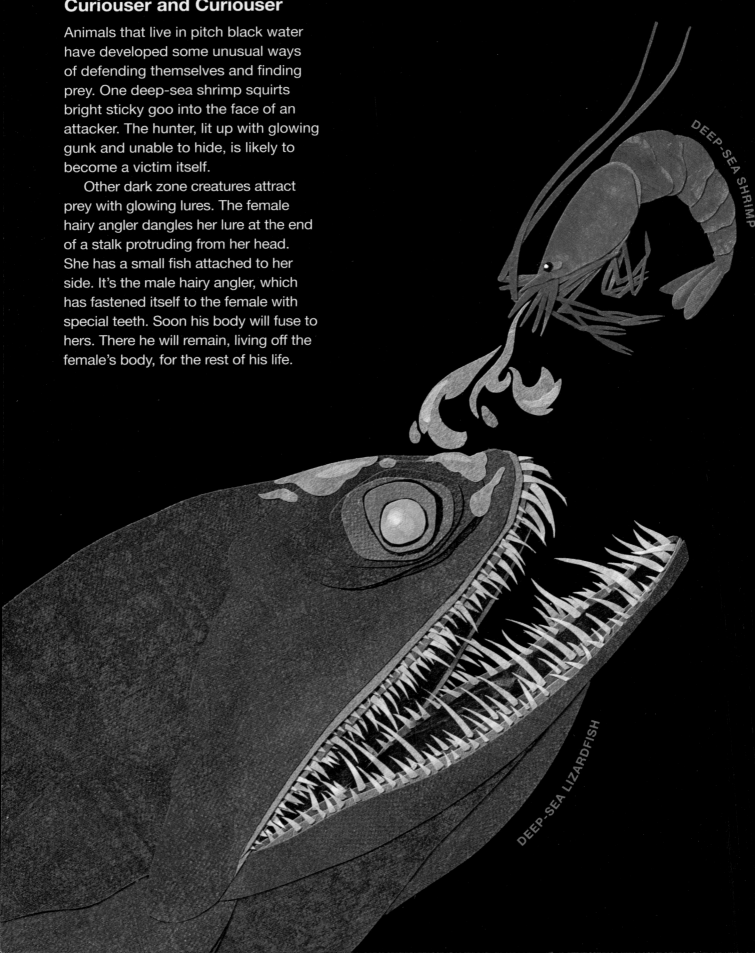

Curiouser and Curiouser

Animals that live in pitch black water have developed some unusual ways of defending themselves and finding prey. One deep-sea shrimp squirts bright sticky goo into the face of an attacker. The hunter, lit up with glowing gunk and unable to hide, is likely to become a victim itself.

Other dark zone creatures attract prey with glowing lures. The female hairy angler dangles her lure at the end of a stalk protruding from her head. She has a small fish attached to her side. It's the male hairy angler, which has fastened itself to the female with special teeth. Soon his body will fuse to hers. There he will remain, living off the female's body, for the rest of his life.

DEEP-SEA SHRIMP

DEEP-SEA LIZARDFISH

5,000 FEET
(1,524 METERS)
41° F (5° C)

MALE AND FEMALE
HAIRY ANGLERS

When Do We Eat?

The water is very cold. We began our descent in warm tropical water, but at these depths the ocean is the same frigid temperature everywhere in the world. The pressure is so great that only a few research vessels can explore here. There are fewer animals to be found, and the ones that do live here may have to go a long time between meals. Unlike the large, fast-swimming predators of the sunlit zone, most animals here are small, and need less food. They ambush their prey, waiting quietly for it to get close, then lunging and grabbing with long, sharp teeth. Some hunters have a stomach that can stretch to many times its normal size, allowing them to swallow an animal that is larger than they are.

LOOSEJAW STOPLIGHT FISH

FANGTOOTH

BLACK SWALLOWER

6,500 FEET •
(1,981 METERS)
36° F (2° C)

Battle of the Giants

The sperm whale is the largest predator on the planet. Like all whales, the sperm whale is a mammal, and it must come to the surface to breathe. As it hunts for giant squid, its favorite food, the sperm whale dives deeper than any other air-breathing animal. When attacked, the giant squid fight back, and many sperm whales are deeply scarred with squid sucker marks. The fierce battles of these giants take place in total darkness, marked only by the bioluminescent flash of deep-sea comb jellies and other small animals.

SPERM WHALE

DEEP-SEA COMB JELLY

10,000 FEET
(3,048 METERS)
36° F (2° C)

GIANT SQUID

Ooze

We have arrived at a flat, nearly featureless surface. It's the abyssal (*ah-**bis**-uhl*) plain. Sediment and marine snow has drifted down from above for millions of years, forming a layer of ooze that may be thousands of feet thick. Most animals here survive by sifting through the mud for bits of food. A few are predators or scavengers, eating other sea floor creatures and larger animals that die and sink to the bottom. Rocky outcrops here and there in the mud provide a habitat for the sea lily — an animal that looks like a plant — and other creatures that attach themselves to hard surfaces.

Soon we'll continue our descent — we have a long way to go before we reach the deepest part of the ocean. But first we'll investigate what looks like a city of smoking towers . . .

SWIMMING SEA CUCUMBER

SEA LILY

TRIPOD FISH

13,000 FEET
(3,962 METERS)
36° F (2° C)

HAGFISH

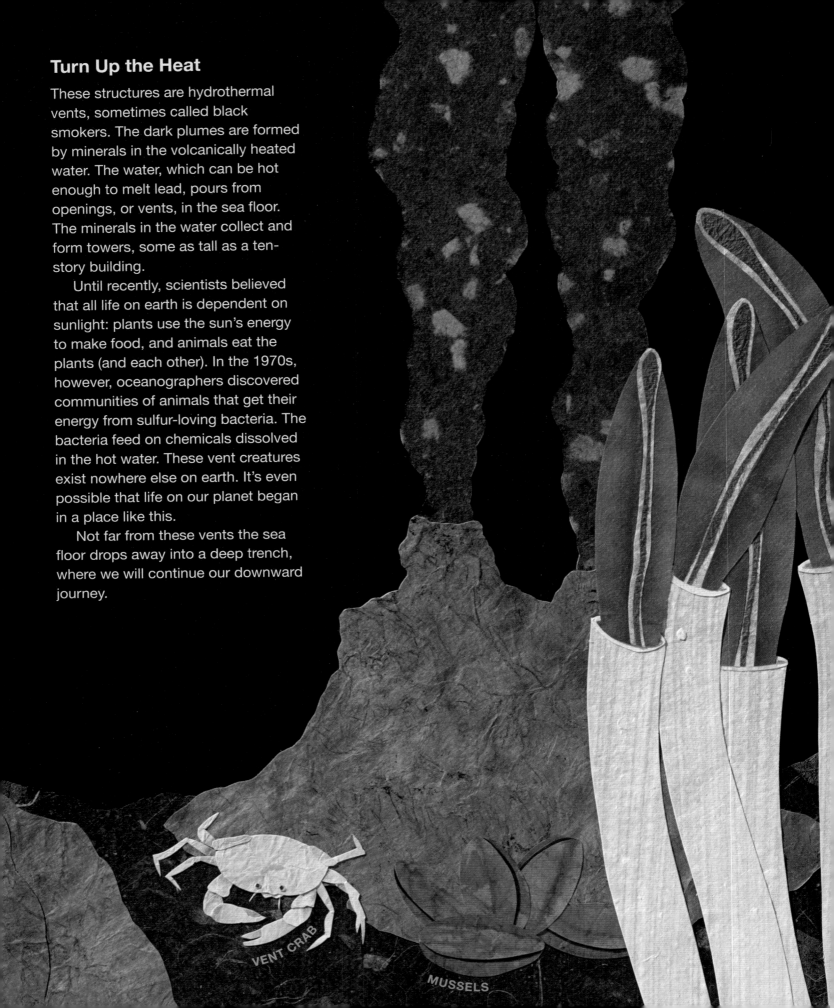

Turn Up the Heat

These structures are hydrothermal vents, sometimes called black smokers. The dark plumes are formed by minerals in the volcanically heated water. The water, which can be hot enough to melt lead, pours from openings, or vents, in the sea floor. The minerals in the water collect and form towers, some as tall as a ten-story building.

Until recently, scientists believed that all life on earth is dependent on sunlight: plants use the sun's energy to make food, and animals eat the plants (and each other). In the 1970s, however, oceanographers discovered communities of animals that get their energy from sulfur-loving bacteria. The bacteria feed on chemicals dissolved in the hot water. These vent creatures exist nowhere else on earth. It's even possible that life on our planet began in a place like this.

Not far from these vents the sea floor drops away into a deep trench, where we will continue our downward journey.

VENT CRAB

MUSSELS

VENT OCTOPUS

13,000 FEET •
(3,962 METERS)
36⁰ F (2⁰ C) TO
750° F (399° C)

GIANT TUBE WORMS

EELPOUT

How Low Can You Go?

Here, at the deepest spot in the sea, there is almost seven miles of water above our heads. This is the Challenger Deep. It is part of the Marianas Trench, a sea floor canyon in the western Pacific Ocean. Humans have visited this place only once. In 1960 the U.S. research vessel *Trieste* reached the sea floor with two scientists aboard. The descent took five hours, but the men stayed on the bottom for only twenty minutes. Unmanned probes have explored the Challenger Deep on a few other occasions, but it is still one of the most remote places on earth. The pressure here is 1,100 times greater than at the surface, and the temperature is a constant 36° F (2° C).

 Even here life can be found. Shrimp, worms, flatfish, and thousands of kinds of bacteria live in the ooze or just above the muddy bottom.

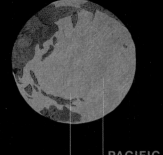

PACIFIC OCEAN
MARIANAS TRENCH

SHRIMP

WORM

FLATFISH

It's time to return to the surface. The trip will take two hours, and except for the lights we've brought along, we will be in complete darkness until the last two minutes or so. Just about every time humans venture into the deep ocean, they discover new and unexpected animals. Some scientists believe that we've seen fewer than half the large animals living in the sea. If we're lucky, we'll encounter some of these unknown creatures on our return trip.

35,838 FEET
(10,923 METERS)
36 °F (2° C)

Here you can find more information about the animals in this book. The diagrams show the size of each of these creatures compared to an adult human's body or hand.

 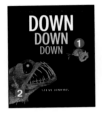

❶ The **hatchet fish** gets its name from the bladelike shape of its body, which is so thin that it almost disappears when viewed head-on. Its huge eyes are fixed in an upward gaze. With them, the hatchet fish hunts for shrimp or small fish silhouetted against the faint light coming from the surface. To protect itself from predators doing the same thing, the hatchet fish has rows of light-producing spots on its belly that can be adjusted to match the light coming from above. Adult hatchet fish are about four inches (10 centimeters) long.

❷ With its snakelike body and frighteningly long teeth, the **viperfish** looks like a real-life sea monster. Because it lives deep in the sea and is only about one foot (30 centimeters) long, the viperfish isn't a threat to humans. It feeds on shrimp, squid, and other fish.

Above the Surface

❶ The **Portuguese man-of-war** drifts across the ocean's surface, its air-filled bladder catching the wind like a sail. Poison tentacles as long as 33 feet (10 meters) trail through the water, snaring small fish and shrimp. These tentacles can give human swimmers painful, even fatal stings. The man-of-war is not a single animal but a colony of many small organisms living and working together. If it is threatened, the man-of-war can deflate its bladder and sink into the water.

❷ The wingspan of the **albatross** reaches 12 feet (3½ meters), the largest of any bird. These graceful seabirds spend months in the air, traveling thousands of miles without landing. They can soar for hours at a time without flapping their wings. Albatrosses feed on fish, squid, and shrimp, scooping them from the surface as they glide just above the waves.

Out of the Water

❶ The **great white shark** is the largest predatory fish in the sea. It reaches 23 feet (7 meters) in length, and can weigh more than three tons (2,720 kilograms). Great whites can detect faint electrical fields created by animals in the water, and have an excellent sense of smell. They also have some 3,000 razor-sharp teeth, arranged in rows. The great white shark can be dangerous to humans — there are a few fatal attacks on swimmers or surfers every year — but its reputation as a vicious man-eater is exaggerated.

❷ **Flying fish** don't actually fly. They escape predators by leaping from the water, spreading their large fins, and gliding. In this way they may travel through the air for hundreds of feet. Flying fish are about one foot (30 centimeters) in length. They gather in schools near the surface and feed on plankton.

❸ Squid suck water in through their gills and force it out of a tube on the underside of their body, propelling themselves through the water. **Flying squid** put on a burst of speed, shoot from the water, and glide through the air for as much as 100 feet (30 meters). Squid eat fish, shrimp, plankton, and other squid. Flying squid can be more than three feet (1 meter) long.

❹ **Spinner dolphins** are air-breathing mammals. They are about the size of a grown man. Spinners swim in groups of hundreds or thousands of dolphins. They use sound to communicate with each other and to locate prey, listening as their clicks and squeaks echo from schools of fish or squid. The acrobatic leaps and twirls that give spinner dolphins their name may be a way to signal others in their group.

It's a Small World

❶ Any small organism that is carried from place to place by ocean currents is called plankton. **Krill** is a kind of animal plankton, or zooplankton (***zo-oh-plank**-tuhn*). Zooplankton includes the larvae of jellyfish, sea stars, urchins, and worms, as well as the eggs of fish and other sea creatures. It ranges in size from microscopic, single-celled creatures to shrimplike animals — including krill — that may be several inches long. Phytoplankton (***fy-toe-plank**-tuhn*) refers to drifting plants, algae, and bacteria that get their energy directly from the sun.

❷ The name **mackerel** is used to describe dozens of different fish species. The largest, the king mackerel, is more than five feet (1½ meters) long. Other mackerel, some just a few inches long, gather in great schools and feed on zooplankton.

Big Fish Eat Little Fish

❶ The **shearwater** gets its name from its habit of flying just above the surface of the ocean. Shearwaters aren't large birds — most are less than 20 inches (51 centimeters) long — but they are champions of long-distance flight, covering as much as 40,000 miles (64,000 kilometers) during their annual migration. Shearwaters are excellent swimmers and reach depths of 180 feet (55 meters) as they dive for fish and squid.

❷ **Bluefin tuna** are fast, powerful open-ocean hunters. They are large fish, reaching ten feet (3 meters) in length and weighing as much as 1,200 pounds (544 kilograms). Bluefins travel in schools and eat fish and squid. Most fish are cold-blooded — their bodies are the same temperature as the water they swim in. The bluefin tuna, however, can raise its body temperature. This allows its muscles to work at full power even in cold water.

❸ **Sailfish** can swim at speeds of 68 miles (109 kilometers) per hour, faster than any other animal. When hunting, the sailfish raises its fin to help herd its prey into a dense ball. The sailfish then swims straight through the mass of fish or squid, stunning or killing many of them with its long bill. Sailfish may reach ten feet (3 meters) in length and 220 pounds (100 kilograms) in weight.

❹ **Green sea turtles** must come to the surface to breathe air, and they build their nests on land. Except for the female turtle's brief trip to the beach to lay her eggs, however, these reptiles spend their entire lives in the ocean. Young turtles feed on jellyfish, but adults eat only seaweed and algae. Green sea turtles grow to five feet (1½ meters) in length and can weigh 575 pounds (261 kilograms).

❺ The **mola mola**, or ocean sunfish, is one of the largest fish in the sea. It may be 10 feet (3 meters) long and weigh as much as 5,000 pounds (2,268 kilograms). The mola mola's diet consists mostly of jellyfish and plankton. It is found in warm water throughout the world's oceans, from the surface to the twilight zone.

Filter Feeders

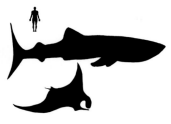

❶ Despite its name, the **whale shark** is not a whale. It is an enormous fish — a shark — with a mouth almost five feet (1½ meters) across. Swimming slowly through plankton-rich waters with its cavernous mouth wide open, it strains millions of tiny animals from the water. Whale sharks eat only plankton and are harmless to humans. The largest whale shark ever captured was 41 feet (12½ meters) long and weighed more than 47,000 pounds (21,300 kilograms).

❷ Rays, like their relatives the sharks, are ancient creatures — they appeared in the oceans around 470 million years ago. The **manta ray,** which can be 25 feet (7½ meters) across and weigh 5,000 pounds (2,268 kilograms), is the largest ray. It gets the nickname "devil ray" from hornlike projections on either side of its face. These are used to funnel plankton and small fish into the ray's mouth, where they are trapped by its gills. The manta ray may look frightening, but it does not threaten people.

Soft Bodies

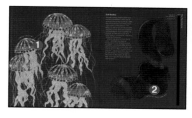

❶ Jellyfish range in size from delicate creatures the size of a hen's egg to giants eight feet (2½ meters) in diameter with tentacles 200 feet (61 meters) long. They are primitive animals — jellyfish drifted in the seas more than 500 million years ago. The **compass jellyfish,** which lives in warm ocean waters throughout the world, is about eight inches (20 centimeters) across, with tentacles two feet (61 centimeters) long. Compass jellyfish feed on plankton and small fish, which they trap with their poisonous tentacles.

❷ The **girdle of Venus** is a comb jelly about three feet (91 centimeters) long. Its body is flat, and so thin and transparent that it is almost invisible as it hovers motionless in the water. It feeds on the plankton that get trapped on its sticky surface.

Visitors from the Deep

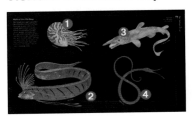

❶ The **chambered nautilus** is the last living member of a family of animals that were the top predators on earth 450 million years ago. Some had shells six and a half feet (2 meters) across. The modern-day nautilus is about eight inches (20 centimeters) in diameter. It eats crabs, shrimp, and fish, and swims by squirting water out of a siphon near its head. Octopuses, sharks, and turtles prey on the nautilus. It defends itself by withdrawing into its shell and covering the opening with a tough, leathery hood.

❷ The **oarfish** grows to lengths of 36 feet (11 meters) or more. It spends most of its time well below the surface and has rarely been seen alive. Humans most often encounter an oarfish after it has died and washed up on the beach. This fish's occasional visits to shallow water, however, may be responsible for some sea monster legends. Despite its dragonlike appearance, the oarfish eats mostly plankton, small fish, and jellyfish.

❸ The most unusual feature of the **goblin shark** is its long snout. Its eyes, unlike those of many of the animals living in the deep sea, are small. Its nose, however, is covered with cells that can sense faint electrical fields in the water. These cells help the shark find fish and squid in the dark water. Goblin sharks, which can be more than ten feet (3 meters) long, push their jaws forward to grasp their prey. Humans normally see this rare deep-water fish only after it has become entangled in a fisherman's net.

❹ The **snipe eel** looks like a piece of ribbon with a bird's head at one end. It has a long beak with tips that curve outward, so it can't close its mouth. Its beak is filled with tiny backwards-pointing teeth. As it swims slowly through the water, the snipe eel's open jaws snag the antennae of shrimp, its favorite food. Snipe eels grow to five feet (1½ meters) in length but weigh only a few ounces.

Glowing in the Dark

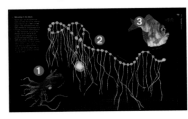

❶ The **vampire squid** has the largest eyes, for its body size, of any animal. Its scientific name means "vampire squid from hell," perhaps because its eight arms are lined with fleshy hooks as well as suckers. Its body, which is about one foot (30 centimeters) long, is covered with light-producing organs. They can be flashed on and off rapidly to confuse prey or predators.

❷ **Siphonophores** (*sahy-fon-uh-fors*) are colonial animals, made up of thousands of individual organisms living together. Deep-sea siphonophores can reach lengths of 130 feet (40 meters). These jelly-like animals are fragile and break into pieces if caught in a net. It wasn't until scientists began exploring the deep ocean in research submarines that they discovered what these creatures really look like. All siphonophores are predators. Those living in deep water attract shrimp, fish, and other small animals with glowing lures and trap them with sticky tentacles.

❸ A **hatchet fish** also appears on the title page. It is described at the beginning of the information section.

It's Snowing!

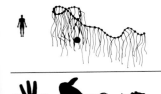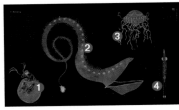

❶ The **pram bug** is a deep-sea amphipod with a frightening, if tiny, set of jaws and claws. Pram bugs are only about one inch (2½ centimeters) long. They lay their eggs in the body of a salp, a jelly-like animal. First the pram bug kills the salp by eating away its insides, leaving a hollow shell. Then it moves in, clinging to the husk of the salp's body with its claws. Here it will make its home, sheltering its eggs and feeding on plankton and bits of marine snow.

❷ The **pelican eel** is a fish, not an eel. It is also known as an umbrellamouth gulper. The pelican eel can unhinge its jaw and swallow fish larger than itself, but like most deep-sea creatures it is not a picky eater, and also consumes shrimp and plankton. Pelican eels grow to about 30 inches (76 centimeters) in length.

❸ The **deep-sea jellyfish** lives in water as deep as 23,000 feet (7,000 meters), but rises to shallower regions to feed on shrimp and plankton. Its body, which is about eight inches (20 centimeters) long, is covered with bioluminescent spots. It often drifts about with its tentacles raised above its body.

❹ The **arrow worm** is a small, nearly transparent creature. Arrow worms that live in deep ocean waters are bioluminescent and are only about one inch (2½ centimeters) long. Arrow worms feed on plankton, which they detect with rows of tiny hairs running along the sides of their body.

Curiouser and Curiouser

1 The bright red **deep-sea shrimp** is about one inch (2½ centimeters) long. It is one of several small creatures that use bioluminescent mucus as a defense against predators. Some leave glowing or flashing swirls in the water to confuse their attacker. Others, including the deep-sea shrimp, shoot it directly into the face of a hunter. These shrimp feed on animal plankton.

2 The **deep-sea lizardfish** is about two feet (61 centimeters) long. Its many needle-sharp teeth are hinged to fold backwards. It doesn't have to swallow its prey — as its victims struggle they work their way farther and farther into the lizardfish's gullet.

3 The female **hairy angler** is about one foot (30 centimeters) long. The male, which lives as a parasite attached to the female's body, is about one-tenth her size. The female's long fleshy antennae detect movement in the water. Her lure, which is filled with bioluminescent bacteria, attracts curious fish and shrimp, which she swallows in one gulp.

When Do We Eat?

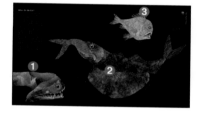 

1 The **loosejaw stoplight fish** has a lower jaw that can be unhinged and an elastic stomach. It can swallow prey larger than its own body. This small fish is about six inches (15 centimeters) long. Most remarkably, it has two patches on its face that produce red light. This light shines forward into the water like a search beam. Few deep-water creatures can see red light. This fish uses its red bioluminescence to find prey — shrimp and amphipods — that don't realize that they are being illuminated.

2 The **black swallower** may hold the record for eating an animal larger than itself — a dead black swallower was found with a fish four times its own length in its stomach. Usually no more than ten inches (25 centimeters) long, the black swallower has sharp, backwards-pointing teeth. It works its victim into its stomach in much the same way as a boa constrictor swallows its prey.

3 The **fangtooth** is also called an ogrefish. It has the largest teeth relative to its body size of any animal. There are special sockets on either side of the fangtooth's brain into which its lower fangs slide when it closes its mouth. Fortunately for us, this fearsome fish is only about six inches (15 centimeters) long.

Battle of the Giants

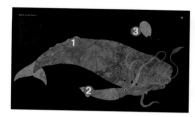 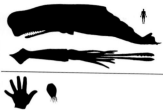

1 The **sperm whale** locates its prey with sound, using a powerful form of animal sonar. Like a bat, the whale produces a series of calls and listens for the echoes. A large male sperm whale may be 60 feet (18 meters) long and weigh 55 tons (50,000 kilograms). With a body specially adapted to withstand tremendous pressure, it can dive to depths 10,000 feet (3,048 meters) and hold its breath for two hours. In a deep dive, the whale's lungs collapse to one one-hundredth of their normal volume. In addition to giant squid, sperm whales eat fish, rays, and smaller squid.

2 **Giant squid** may reach 60 feet (18 meters) in length. A dead squid can be stretched when it's laid out and measured, and there is disagreement among scientists about just how long this animal really is. The giant squid has a powerful beak and ten tentacles. Two of the tentacles, much longer than the others, can be extended quickly to grab prey. The giant squid eats fish, rays, and other squid. No one had ever seen this animal alive until 2004, when Japanese scientists in a submarine sighted one.

3 **Comb jellies** have lived in the sea for a long time — we've unearthed fossil imprints of these animals more than 500 million years old. Comb jellies are not closely related to jellyfish, and do not have stinging cells. Like jellyfish, however, they are predators, snaring animal plankton with their sticky bodies and tentacles. They are found from the surface to water several miles deep. Most comb jellies are small, not more than a few inches long. Some scientists think that there are more comb jellies than any other animal in the world.

Ooze

1 Most sea cucumbers crawl along on the bottom of the ocean, but the **swimming sea cucumber** undulates its body and moves gracefully above the sea floor as it feeds on bits of decaying food and marine snow. When it is threatened, the sea cucumber lights up its entire surface with bioluminescence, then sheds its glowing skin to confuse its attacker. Swimming sea cucumbers reach 12 inches (30 centimeters) in length.

2 The **tripod fish** spends most of its time resting on the sea floor, balanced on three elongated fins. It faces into the current and eats animal plankton drifting past. Tripod fish grow to be about 12 inches (30 centimeters) long.

❸ Despite its name and appearance, the **sea lily** is an animal. It anchors itself to hard surfaces with a plantlike stalk and uses feathery arms to filter bits of food from the water. Sea lilies grow to a height of 24 inches (61 centimeters). When danger threatens, they can leave their stalk behind and crawl slowly across the sea floor.

❹ The skin of the **hagfish,** or slime eel, can produce enough mucus to choke an attacker. Hagfish, which rely on an acute sense of smell, feed on both living and dead animals, often entering through a victim's mouth and eating it from the inside out. They average about 18 inches (46 centimeters) in length.

Turn Up the Heat

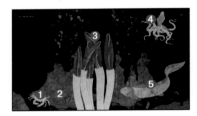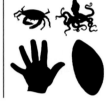

Communities of hydrothermal vent animals are dependent on sulfur-loving bacteria. These bacteria thrive on minerals dissolved in volcanically heated water that pours from openings in the sea floor. Some vent animals, including ❶ **vent crabs,** ❷ **mussels,** and ❸ **giant tube worms,** eat these bacteria. Others, such as the ❹ **vent octopus** and the ❺ **eelpout,** a snakelike fish, feed on the bacteria-eating animals. Many of these animals are small, no more than a few inches in length. Giant tube worms, however, can be ten feet (3 meters) tall.

How Low Can You Go?

❶ **Shrimp,** ❷ **worms,** and at least one kind of ❸ **flatfish** live at the bottom of the Marianas Trench. These animals were either observed by the scientists who traveled there or photographed by unmanned probes. We don't know a lot about the animals that live in the deepest part of the ocean, but we know that some creatures do manage to thrive there. No doubt there are other animals living at these depths that no human has ever seen.

Bibliography

In the Deep Sea.
By Sneed B. Collard III. Marshall Cavendish Benchmark, 2006.
Ocean: A Visual Guide.
By Stephen Hutchinson and Lawrence E. Hawkins. Firefly Books, 2005.
The Deep.
By Claire Nouvian. University of Chicago Press, 2007.
The Oceans.
By Ellen J. Prager. McGraw Hill, 2000.
The Universe Below.
By William J. Broad. Simon & Schuster, 1998.

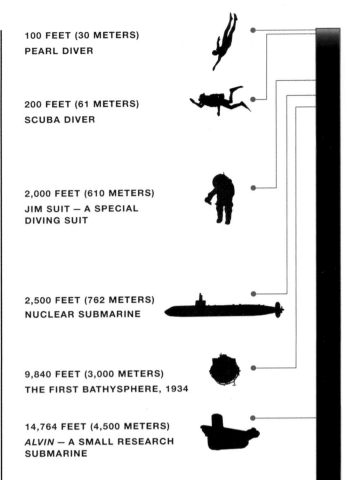

100 FEET (30 METERS)
PEARL DIVER

200 FEET (61 METERS)
SCUBA DIVER

2,000 FEET (610 METERS)
JIM SUIT — A SPECIAL DIVING SUIT

2,500 FEET (762 METERS)
NUCLEAR SUBMARINE

9,840 FEET (3,000 METERS)
THE FIRST BATHYSPHERE, 1934

14,764 FEET (4,500 METERS)
***ALVIN* — A SMALL RESEARCH SUBMARINE**

35,838 FEET (10,923 METERS)
***TRIESTE* — THE FIRST VESSEL TO REACH THE DEEPEST SPOT IN THE OCEAN**